JAPANESE

Michio Fujioka

Photographs by
Kazunori Tsunenari

Translated by H. Mack Horton

RESIDENCES
AND
GARDENS
A Tradition of Integration

KODANSHA INTERNATIONAL LTD.
Tokyo, New York, and San Francisco

Half-title page: Bush Clover Court, Kyoto Imperial Palace.
Title page: Seiryōden, Kyoto Imperial Palace.
Contents page: Shishinden viewed from the Jōmeimon gate,
Kyoto Imperial Palace.

Note to the Reader: Japanese names in the text are given in the
customary Japanese order, surname preceding given name.

The publishers are indebted to the Izumi Metropolitan Kubo Sō
Memorial Art Gallery, Benrido Company, Ltd., and Messrs.
Michio Fujioka and Kazunori Tsunenari for providing black-and-
white photographs.

Distributed in the United States by Kodansha International/
USA, Ltd. through Harper & Row, Publishers, Inc., 10 East 53rd
Street, New York, New York 10022.

Published by Kodansha International Ltd., 2-2, Otowa 1-
chome, Bunkyo-ku, Tokyo 112 and Kodansha International/
USA Ltd., 10 East 53rd Street, New York, New York 10022 and
The Hearst Building, 5 Third Street, Suite 400, San Francisco,
California 94103

LCC 82-18660
ISBN 0-87011-561-8 (U.S.)
ISBN 4-7700-1056-7 (in Japan)

Library of Congress Cataloging in Publication Data
Fujioka, Michio, 1908-
    Japanese residences and gardens.

    (Great Japanese art)
    Bibliography: p.
    1. Architecture, Domestic—Japan. 2. Gardens,
    Japanese. I. Title. II. Series.
NA7451.F728 1982   728.8'0952   82-18660
ISBN 0-87011-561-8 (U.S.)

14,5 24

CONTENTS

1. Shishinden, Kyoto Imperial Palace.

2. Tsune Goten and plum, Kyoto Imperial Palace.

3. Kogosho and Gogakumonsho, Kyoto Imperial Palace.

4. Chōsetsu interior, Kyoto Imperial Palace.

5. Chōsetsu, Kyoto Imperial Palace.

◁6. Garden, Sentō Palace (overleaf).

7. Seikatei teahouse, Sentō Palace.

8. Ninomaru Palace garden, Nijō Castle.

10. Veranda and railing of the New Palace, Katsura Detached Palace.

9. Stone path and Palanquin Entry, Katsura Detached Palace.

11. Shoin complex, Katsura Detached Palace (overleaf). ▷

◁12. Shōkintei teahouse, Katsura Detached Palace (overleaf).

14. Hearth of the Shōkintei teahouse, Katsura Detached Palace.

13. Shōkintei teahouse, Katsura Detached Palace.

◁15. Yokuryūchi pond and Rin'untei teahouse, Shugakuin Detached Palace (overleaf).

16. Rinshunkaku, Sankeien.

17. Interior of Building Two of the Rinshunkaku, Sankeien.

18. Ōhiroma and Reclining Dragon pine of the Sumiya.

19. Garden court of the Sumiya.

Japanese Residences and Gardens: A Tradition of Integration

JAPANESE DWELLINGS AND THE NATURAL WORLD

The Japanese have traditionally cherished their natural environment and cultivated a unique harmony between their surroundings and their way of life. This symbiosis was fostered in part by Japan's temperate climate. Admittedly, the Japanese archipelago reaches far to the north and south and includes subtropic areas as well as places with abundant snowfall. But the central section of the nation, where the bulk of the population settled and which became the country's cultural heartland, has in general not been prey to extremes of temperature. This, together with its adequate rainfall, has made central Japan particularly well suited to human habitation. There the seasons are a feast for the eye—in spring the cherry blossoms delight passersby, and in the fall the reds and yellows of the foliage transform the mountainsides.

To describe the historical changes that have taken place in the spatial relationship between Japanese architecture and the natural world, we should look first at the aristocratic mansions of the Heian period (794–1185), the age in which imported Chinese culture was gradually imbued with a unique Japanese character. In the latter half of this elegant and peaceful era, from about the later tenth to the early twelfth centuries, the *shinden* style of architecture—probably the most thoroughly Japanese of any style in the country's history—became the accepted one for aristocratic mansions. The ideal shinden complex was located on a site measuring about one hundred meters square. In the center, facing south, stood the main building, the shinden, which served as the living quarters of the head of the household as well as the site of ceremonials and entertainment (fig. 1). Connected by corridors to the east and/or west were *tai-no-ya*, secondary structures in which the rest of the family lived and whose longer axes were oriented north to south. A corridor, or corridors (*chūmonrō*), broken in the middle by gates (*chūmon*), extended south from these tai-no-ya, and ended in small "fishing pavilions" (*tsuridono*) that overlooked a pond. This pond, fed by a stream running from behind the shinden to the north, filled the southern part of the complex and included

an island reached by a vermilion bridge. The Heian capital (present-day Kyoto) had numerous springs at that time, which helped make this type of pond construction possible. The earth dug to create the pond was used to fashion a hillock to the south, which was then planted with a variety of trees that would blossom at various times during the year.

The shinden did not have bearing walls; instead it was by and large enclosed with reticulated shutters (*shitomido*). Each shutter was composed of an upper and a lower part and was opened by swinging the top half upward and fastening it to the eave above; the lower half was then lifted out of its grooves in the posts to both sides. Swinging double doors (*tsumado*) of solid planking were added at the building's sides for egress when the shutters were closed. Behind the shutters were hung blinds (*misu*) made of thin strips of bamboo threaded together. When the shutters were opened and blinds rolled up, a continuum between interior and exterior space was created. When it snowed, for example, the white garden landscape could be enjoyed from

Fig. 1. Model of shinden complex.

Fig. 2. Illustration of a garden in a shinden complex (from *Komakurabe Gyōkō Emaki* [*An Imperial Visit to the Horse Race*]). Izumi Metropolitan Kubo Sō Memorial Art Gallery.

within the house. In like manner, the carp in the pond could be viewed or caught from the fishing pavilion. The surrounding nature could also be enjoyed, and poems to it recited, while boating on the pond or while sitting on the hillock under its blossoming trees (fig. 2).

Of course, traditional European architecture too shows a high regard for the natural world. In the northern regions of the continent, it is true, this is difficult to express in terms of intimacy between structure and garden. Buildings are traditionally constructed with thick stone walls and small windows so as to provide shelter from the cold. When a garden is laid out, therefore, it usually remains independent and is not fully integrated with the building proper. In the more temperate areas of the Mediterranean, on the other hand, there are courtyards incorporated into the buildings themselves and filled to overflowing with potted plants, which are aligned in rows on the floor, hung from walls, or otherwise arranged. From early times, in the expansive Roman villas at Pompeii and Ostia, for instance, there are remnants of inner courtyards that once contained gardens and springs. Though these would seem to approach the attitude toward nature evinced in the shinden complex, they are still quite different in that their gardens were never meant to seem other than man-made. To be sure, the shinden garden is equally artificial, but it is designed to appear a reduced version of nature in its pristine state. A harmony between the residence and the natural world *as it is* thus develops.

The Heian aristocrats also introduced nature into the interiors of their dwellings in the form of screen paintings of famous scenic spots in various of the country's provinces and extolled their natural beauty in poetry. Since transportation remained relatively primitive at this time, it was impossible for the nobility to travel frequently or easily. They therefore sent painters to spots famed for their beauty and had them execute screens that the aristocrats could enjoy at home.

This love of nature is seen even today in Japanese houses built in the traditional style. When the glass doors bordering their verandas are opened, a continuity between the interior and the garden is established. Thus, though it must be admitted that with the extreme spatial limitations on modern urban and suburban structures the sense of oneness with the surrounding natural environment is unavoidably diminished, these homes stand at the end of an unbroken architectural lineage.

TRADITION IN THE KYOTO IMPERIAL PALACE

The Imperial Palace in Japan's ancient capital, Kyoto, provides a fine example of the unity of interior and exterior space that characterizes traditional Japanese architecture (figs. 3, 4). The palace was rebuilt in several different styles during its long history, and today it stands in a somewhat different location from that of the original. So too has the number of constituent structures varied over time. But in the reconstruction at the end of the eighteenth century, the ceremonial sections of the complex were restored to their Heian configurations. Although the exteriors were designed by late eighteenth-century builders and cannot be uncritically assumed to be pure Heian reconstructions, the plan of the complex was carefully worked out to reflect as closely as possible Heian design concepts. For our purposes here, the present palace can be thought of as a close approximation of the original.

The main hall of the Imperial Palace is the Shishinden (or Shishiiden; pl. 1). Before it stretches an expansive courtyard spread with white gravel, at the front of which stands the Jōmeimon gate (see contents page). It was in the Shishinden that the most important state ceremonies took place. When a new emperor underwent the ceremony of accession, for example,

Fig. 3. Kyoto Imperial Palace seen from the southwest, with Mount Hiei in distance at right.

Fig. 4. Partial view of Kyoto Imperial Palace: Shishinden in center facing Jōmeimon gate, Seiryōden at right, Kogosho at left.

the gravel-covered courtyard served as a kind of outdoor room, and as such functioned as an integral part of the Shishinden structure. Though the cherry tree and orange tree planted to either side of the front steps of the hall lend it a floral note, the space, surrounded as it is by corridors and subsidiary structures, is less important as a garden than as a place for formal observances. So important was it to court ceremonial that in the early years of the Heian period inclement weather would force an event to be cancelled. This was not the case, though, for ceremonies held in other palace buildings, which were not cancelled when it rained, but only changed in content. These "rain ceremonies" (ugi) gradually became the norm regardless of the weather.

The Shishinden is built by and large of unpainted wood, with cypress-bark roofing. Overt decoration is in general avoided, save for very understated black lacquering on the shutters and vermilion lacquering on the metal fixtures. Compared to the luxury of the royal residences in Europe, the Shishinden is simplicity itself. This holds as well in comparison to Chinese imperial palaces, which, though also built of wood, are painted with a dazzling array of colors. The understatement of the Shishinden is obvious even in comparison to other Japanese structures, most notably the Ninomaru Palace of Nijō Castle, Kyoto residence of the Tokugawa shoguns (figs. 9–11). The Ninomaru Palace boasts intricately carved transoms (ramma), golden wall and screen paintings, and colorful and complex designs on even its ceiling coffers. One possible reason for the simplicity of the Imperial Palace is that as opposed to the absolute power of some European monarchs, the Japanese emperor throughout most of the Heian period was more or less a symbolic figure, and had neither the need for architecture designed to express his power nor the ability to exploit the populace for construction funds.

THE DEVELOPMENT OF GARDEN COURTS

Because the shinden complex was composed of a number of buildings connected by corridors, small enclosed spaces were created *ipso facto* by the design. A number of these small garden courtyards (*tsuboniwa*) are found in the Imperial Palace, though not always in their original configurations. For example, the Seiryōden hall (see title page), situated to the west of the Shishinden, served in part as a day-to-day living area of the emperor. In the seventeenth century, however, the emperors took up residence in the Tsune Goten palace (pl. 2), and the Seiryōden became a ceremonial hall, second in importance to the Shishinden. When the Imperial Palace complex was restored in the late eighteenth century to its Heian configuration, the Seiryōden was rebuilt in the style of Heian ceremonial buildings. Today, a gravelled courtyard abuts on the east facade of the Seiryōden, and two bamboo plants, known as the Kuretake and the Kawatake, stand directly in front of the structure. The reason for this surprising design is that in the Heian period, another building, the Jijūden, was located behind the Shishinden, where the Seiryōden courtyard is now. There was only a limited amount of space between the Seiryōden and the Jijūden, and the two bamboo effectively filled it. The significance from a design standpoint of the two bamboo cannot be appreciated without mentally reconstructing the configuration of the constituent buildings. When this is done, it becomes clear that the long and narrow gravel courtyard with its two bamboo was designed to lend a visual "breath of fresh air" to viewers in the Seiryōden.

Gardens at the Imperial Palace, such as the bamboo courtyard, have regularly been composed of a single type of flora. The most famous of these is the Bush Clover Court (Hagitsubo) on the west side of the complex behind the Seiryōden (see half-

Fig. 5. Higyōsha and Wisteria Court, Kyoto Imperial Palace.

Fig. 6. Kogosho, Kyoto Imperial Palace.

title page). It was at the west side of this hall that the emperor's personal living area was located, as well as those of his female attendants. The bush clover, designed to be viewed from these rooms and surrounded by corridors, were planted in a completely natural arrangement which consciously avoids any hint of artificial regularity. The simple setting is particularly effective during the months when the clover is in bloom. Viewed from within the Seiryōden, the bush clover fulfill the same design function that potted plants might, placed inside a living area.

Another building in the compound with an enclosed garden is the Higyōsha (fig. 5), located far in the rear of the palace. It is here that the ceremony installing a new imperial consort is held. The building was constructed during the eighteenth-century restoration of the palace to its Heian format, and its garden, surrounded by a fence, contains a single wisteria (*fuji*). The garden is therefore known as the Wisteria Court (Fujitsubo). In the Heian period, there had been a block of connected apartments resembling this one, and each opened onto a garden with a different type of vegetation, such as the Paulownia Court (Kiritsubo). These were not rebuilt during the restoration, however. The taste for extreme simplicity that is exemplified in these small, enclosed gardens with their one spot of color appears again in the late fifteenth century with the birth of "tea taste," an aesthetic philosophy that extolled the beauty of a single flower displayed in the decorative alcove (*tokonoma*) of a tearoom.

The Tsune Goten palace (pl. 2), the living area of the emperor, was built as an independent structure for the first time in the seventeenth century. Hitherto the emperor's rooms had been included in the Seiryōden. Although the interior of the Tsune Goten was designed to reflect contemporary, post-shinden designs, the exterior retains the earlier, Heian-period appearance. Even the two plum trees located beside the central stairs—red to one side, white to the other—which can be seen as an imitation of the cherry and orange trees now standing in front of the Shishinden, are more likely a conscious restatement of an earlier Shishinden landscape scheme that used plums to either side of the stairs.

THE IMPERIAL PALACE'S BLEND OF OLD AND NEW

The Kyoto Imperial Palace has a long history, and while it retains its old, traditional configuration, various of its elements show the influences of later architectural ideas. In the rebuilding of the late eighteenth century, for example, certain sections of the palace, those in which formal ceremonies were held, were restored to their Heian appearance in order to better suit the traditional character of the ceremonies themselves. The rooms in which the emperor carried out daily activities, however, were based on contemporary architectural designs. In order to avoid the unpleasant disharmony that would have been caused by a direct juxtaposition of the two styles, an intermediate area incorporating old and new elements was added to modulate the shift. This stylistic blending can be seen in the Kogosho (pl. 3), a building which served a variety of purposes.

The Kogosho, first constructed at the end of the fourteenth century, was subsequently altered in configuration to keep pace with the different uses to which it was put over the years. The form of the present building was established in the late eighteenth century, but the structure itself was rebuilt after fire destroyed the original. Though the interior of the Kogosho shows the influence of the residential style of the seventeenth century, the exterior is much more strongly related to the older shinden type. A garden abuts on the main facade of the structure at the east, and it includes a pond, in keeping with shinden landscape concepts (fig. 6). The design of the pond, how-

Fig. 7. Corridor from Osuzumisho to Chōsetsu, Kyoto Imperial Palace.

Fig. 8. View of garden from sitting room, Chōsetsu, Kyoto Imperial Palace.

ever, no longer reflects Heian prototypes. It instead shows the influence of the late seventeenth century in the flat stones set at the water's edge, which are arranged to suggest a sand-covered seashore. This scheme was standard at the time, and similar types are found at the Retired Emperor's Palace (Sentō Gosho) and at Katsura Detached Palace (Katsura Rikyū). The large number of rocks at the pond's banks is also characteristic of seventeenth-century garden work. These later ideas blend with the building's earlier shinden elements to create a unified whole.

This stylistic confluence is also seen in the design of the island located off the sandy shoreline. The very existence of an island harkens back to shinden ideas. But the bridge leading to it is not a vermilion-lacquered wooden one—as we would expect in a shinden design—but is instead made of stone. The abundance of rocks at the island's banks is also a post-shinden landscape characteristic. The close relationship between house and garden, however, constitutes a direct tie to traditional Japanese architectural philosophy.

Also in evidence at the Kogosho is the principle of "borrowed scenery" (shakkei). The building's eastern facade looks over the front garden and beyond to Kyoto's Eastern Hills (Higashiyama) and incorporates them into the overall design scheme.

Another building in the Imperial Palace complex that shows a blend of old and new is that named "Listening to the Snow" (Chōsetsu; pl. 5). The name, implying a place for appreciating a snowy landscape, perhaps relates to the sound made when, in an otherwise silent landscape, snow piled on tree limbs suddenly falls to the ground. The view of the garden from the sitting room (zashiki) of the Chōsetsu is quite unexceptional until the snow falls, when it is transformed by the white splendor of the garden scenery (fig. 8). The building is con-

structed in the sukiya style, a simple and relaxed architectural type that developed in the seventeenth century through a blending of the shoin style with that of the teahouse. From the shoin style come the decorative alcove (tokonoma) and subsidiary alcove with upper and lower cabinets, the interior sliding partitions (fusuma) and exterior translucent sliding screens (shōji), and the woven straw mats (tatami) (pl. 4). We will see the style in its more formal cast further on at the Ninomaru Palace of Nijō Castle.

The shoin elements in the Chōsetsu have been tempered by the ideals of the tea ceremony, such as the well-known "elegant simplicity" (wabi) and "beauty in imperfection" (sabi). These concepts are given concrete form in the partially unplaned post at the side of the decorative alcove, and in the imaginative and even fanciful design of the subsidiary alcove, with its complex mullion pattern and lack of the traditional shelves found in the more formal shoin conceptions. On the outside, the Chōsetsu includes the veranda typical of shoin works, here running from east to west along the front. But the design has been rendered more genial and informal through the deletion of all posts save those at the veranda corners.

One more noteworthy aspect of the Chōsetsu is seen in the stream that has been channelled under the veranda's southeast corner (pl. 5). This stream runs along the back of the garden hillock and under the corridor leading from another shoin-style structure, the Osuzumisho (fig. 7), an area to which the emperor retired to escape the heat. Directing a stream underneath a corridor was a standard shinden-style design concept, and this, plus the dialogue the stream initiates between the building and the garden, shows the debt the Chōsetsu owes to earlier architectural principles.

Fig. 9. Broad veranda, or corridor, in Tōzamurai, Ninomaru Palace, Nijō Castle.

Fig. 10. Chokushi no Ma of Tōzamurai, Ninomaru Palace, Nijō Castle.

THE ARCHITECTURE AND GARDENS OF THE SENTŌ PALACE

The Sentō Palace was the residence of retired emperors (*jōkō*). This is indicated in the name itself, which means "transcendent's grotto." In the last century it has been the custom for the emperor not to abdicate, but in the past he did so with relative freedom, relinquishing the throne to the crown prince. There were also times when no retired emperor was alive, and others when several were living. Consequently, there was no one palace used consistently by emperors in retirement. The present Sentō Palace was established for the emperor Gomizunoo (1596–1680, r. 1611–29) on his abdication, and it dates from the former half of the seventeenth century. During Gomizunoo's reign, his consort, later known as Tōfukumon'in (1607–78), resided in a separate spacious palace of her own located within the Imperial Palace complex. This division of living areas was to occur again in the construction of the Sentō Palace. Tōfukumon'in was afforded this special privilege by the shogunate because her father was Hidetada (1579–1632), the second of the Tokugawa shoguns.

The Sentō Palace is unique in containing two separate residences and two gardens, one for the retired Gomizunoo and one for Tōfukumon'in, both on the same scale and within the same complex. But although clear evidence remains showing the ponds to have been initially separate, they were later joined by a narrow waterway. These two ponds were divided not only in terms of position, but in style as well. As the original buildings are no longer extant, we cannot determine the stylistic relationships between the architecture and the gardens. But we are sure that the style of Tōfukumon'in's garden itself is original (pl. 6). It is basically designed in the style of the Heian period, but with a number of later elements added, such as gently curved banks and various rock groupings. Another later

characteristic is the garden path around the pond which allows one to appreciate the landscape from different locations while wandering along it. Tōfukumon'in's garden is consequently referred to as a "stroll garden" (*kaiyūshiki teien*). But the overall expansive quality of the conception is characteristic of the Heian garden, as well as the impression it gives of being virgin nature on a reduced scale. The view of the garden from Tōfukumon'in's palace, no longer on the site, must have been a serene one indeed, with the pond enclosed by flowering trees. It is a landscape well suited to feminine taste.

Quite different is Gomizunoo's garden, a famous work by Kobori Enshū, a brilliant designer and accomplished man of taste, as well as a daimyo in his own right. The garden was situated in front of the palace and included a pond with an island. The pond was designed in a style new for the period, and was surrounded by cut stones set out in a rectilinear arrangement. Both garden and palace have been extensively remodelled since their original construction, and today a small section of the pond bank and cut stones are all that remain of the original landscaping. Plate 7 depicts the later design, with the rocks on the pond bank rearranged to suggest the seashore. This is a stereotyped conception and resembles that of the front garden of the Kogosho. The island in the pond is composed of rocks of various sizes. The pavilion in the foreground, called the Seikatei, is designed in a light and open sukiya style and seems to melt into the expansive depths of the garden.

NINOMARU PALACE OF NIJŌ CASTLE—SYMBOL OF THE SHOGUNATE

Nijō Castle was built as the residence of the Tokugawa shogun when he travelled to the capital, Kyoto. While he normally lived in Edo (now Tokyo) and wielded his power from his castle there, on rare occasions the shogun had an audience in Kyoto with the reigning yet virtually powerless emperor when

Fig. 11. Audience hall of Ōhiroma, Ninomaru Palace, Nijō Castle.

a new shogun was installed and at other times established by custom. As opposed to the Imperial Palace, which lacked any means of protection save its earthen wall, the shogun's Nijō Castle was equipped with moats and stone walls for defense. But because Nijō Castle was meant as only a short-term residence, and because it was located in the heart of Kyoto, quite near the Imperial Palace, its design was somewhat different from most other castles, which were built with defense their primary purpose. Nijō might better be considered a residence with defensive appointments. Nevertheless, the difference between the shogun and the emperor is manifest in that of their dwellings.

Within the castle confines stands a shoin complex called the Ninomaru (Second Compound) Palace, arranged on a stepped plan (fig. 12) with the Ōhiroma, the hall for the most formal shogunal interviews, at the center (upper left, pl. 8). To the right (southeast) of the Ōhiroma in the illustration is the Shikidai no Ma, and then the Tōzamurai, the waiting area for daimyos summoned by the shogun. To the left (northwest) is the Kuroshoin, used as a second hall for audiences with the shogun, then his private living area, the Shiroshoin (neither visible in the plate). To the south of this zigzag shoin complex is a magnificent garden with massive rocks set on the banks. It is thought the pond was constructed on such a scale because of a spring conveniently located on the site since the Heian period. Thanks to the stepped plan of the shoin complex this garden can be viewed from each of the palace's structures. Though attributed to the daimyo-designer Kobori Enshū, the garden exhibits a form standard for the seventeenth century. It does not resemble Enshū's design for the garden of Tōfukumon'in at Sentō Palace, introduced earlier in these pages (pl. 6).

The interior of the Ninomaru Palace is one of dazzling splendor, with screens of gold and polychrome, coved and

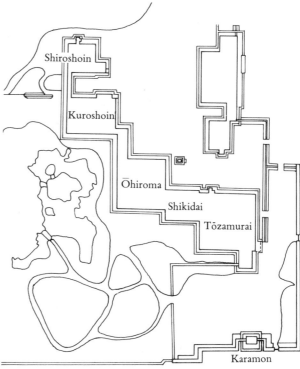

Fig. 12. Plan of Ninomaru Palace, Nijō Castle.

coffered ceilings, and intricately carved and painted transoms (figs. 9–11). It has a different atmosphere entirely from the simplicity and restraint found in the Kyoto Imperial Palace. This impressive decor was necessitated by the shogun's need to emphasize his power and awe his minions.

THE VOGUE FOR COUNTRY VILLAS

With the coming of peace in the seventeenth century, many nobles and daimyo lords began constructing "detached villas" (bessō). Previous to this time it had been impossible for even

Fig. 13. Shoin complex of Katsura Detached Palace. From right: Old Shoin, Middle Shoin, New Palace.

the great warlords Toyotomi Hideyoshi (1536 [37?]–98) and Tokugawa Ieyasu (1542–1616) to build country estates because of the ravages of civil war. These men, who had attained preeminence through military force, were limited to building enclosed areas called "rural compounds" (*yamazatomaru*) within their castles, where they could take their leisure. These rural compounds were designed to re-create the natural world beyond the castle walls, and they provided spiritual respite to people whose time within their fastnesses was spent for the most part in opulent palace rooms lavishly decorated in gold and polychrome. The country was still fraught with too much strife for these men who lived by the sword to build estates beyond the protection of moats and stone walls.

The style of architecture in the rural compounds was based on "tea taste," the aesthetic philosophy embracing rustic simplicity and restraint that was reaching maturity at this time. These gardens inspired in those walking within them a feeling of the great outdoors, a taste we have already suggested to have been inherent not only in the medieval military class but in Japanese of all strata and periods.

The victory of Tokugawa Ieyasu over the last of his rivals in the early seventeenth century initiated a period of peace that was to last for the next two and a half centuries. Two of the first country villas to be built during the new era of tranquility were the Katsura Detached Palace of the princes Hachijō and the Shugakuin Detached Palace of Retired Emperor Gomizunoo. The shogunate, however, kept a firm hand on the activities of the imperial family. Whenever Gomizunoo travelled to the Shugakuin he was accompanied by guards, ostensibly for his benefit, who had been appointed by the shogunal deputy in Kyoto. The retired emperor was irked by these limitations on his freedom, and he appealed to the shogunate to end them, arguing that unlike the shogunate, the nobility was borne no

antipathy by the people, and that the imperial family therefore had no need of protection. The shogunal guards were dismissed thereafter. It may also be for this reason that the first villas were built by nobles, not the military. But various daimyo lords began building retreats in their home provinces soon thereafter.

THE BEAUTY OF THE KATSURA PALACE

The elegance and harmony of Katsura Palace's architecture and gardens is world famous. The palace was begun in the early part of the seventeenth century by Toshihito (1579–1629), the first prince to hold the surname Hachijō. But as the income of noble families was at the time quite small, the first Katsura palace is thought to have been an unassuming structure. Country estates had been located on the same spot in southwest Kyoto since the early eleventh century, during the ascendency of the Fujiwara family, and the configuration of Toshihito's villa may have been influenced by the remains of earlier designs.

It was under the direction of Toshihito's son, Toshitada (1619–62), that Katsura Palace approached its present form. Since Toshitada was married to a daughter of the Maeda family, daimyos second in power only to the Tokugawa themselves, he is thought to have received financial support for his project from his wealthy in-laws. It would have been impossible to construct a complex on Katsura's present scale with the slender resources of nobles at that time. To this financial backing, Toshitada added the aesthetic sensibility for which he and his father were even at the time well known. We have a variety of evidence suggesting that both men went often to the construction site in person to direct work on what was to become the finest of Japan's estates.

Though the villa by and large assumed its present shape under the direction of Toshitada, the project was not brought to

Fig. 14. Shoin complex of Katsura Detached Palace. From left: New Palace, Musical Instrument Room, Middle Shoin, Old Shoin.

Fig. 15. View of garden from Moon-viewing Platform of Old Shoin, Katsura Detached Palace.

a final conclusion until some years later. Katsura is thus the product of several decades of labor. Its design was not fully planned from the first, but instead developed through a process of artistic accretion. Though the overall conception is one of exemplary harmony between the buildings and their natural surroundings, there are several elements of some disunity that unavoidably resulted from expansion and remodelling.

The shoin section of the complex, which was the living area of the palace, is arranged in a stepped plan facing southeast (pl. 11; fig. 16). The section to the far right in our illustration, on the higher ground, is the Old Shoin, built by the elder Prince Hachijō. This is the oldest structure on the estate and was accompanied by a few simple teahouses that no longer exist. The large pond in front was also built in Toshihito's time, but is thought to have been based on remnants of an eleventh-century design and is somewhat Heian in flavor.

To the left of the Old Shoin is the Middle Shoin, built by the second Prince Hachijō, and at the far left is the Musical Instrument Room and then the New Palace. Evidence discovered during recent repairs shows the last two structures to have been built in preparation for the second visit of Retired Emperor Gomizunoo to the premises in 1663. The ground beneath the Middle Shoin and the New Palace is somewhat lower than that of the Old Shoin, and because of the occasional flooding of the nearby Katsura River the foundation walls beneath the verandas were built higher off the ground than usual. This construction is unique to the Katsura Palace. The cypress roofs, papered sliding screens, wooden uprights, and foundation walls with vertical bamboo grillwork (fig. 14) combine in a model of balance and harmony.

Just as the shoin structures show variations in style, so does the view of the garden differ according to the vantage point. The Old Shoin is the simplest of the structures, but its garden

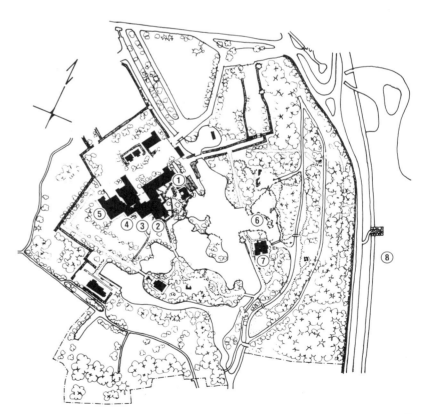

Fig. 16. Plan of Katsura Detached Palace: 1) path to Palanquin Entry, 2) Old Shoin, 3) Middle Shoin, 4) Musical Instrument Room, 5) New Palace, 6) Ama no Hashidate, 7) Shōkintei, 8) Katsura River.

view, with the pond in the foreground and the islands beyond, is the most impressive (fig. 15). The reverse is true for the New Palace. Because it was built for an imperial visit, it eschews the extremely simple materials used in the other buildings in favor of exotic imported woods and delicate metal fixtures, which

Fig. 17. Ichi no Ma of New Palace, Katsura Detached Palace.

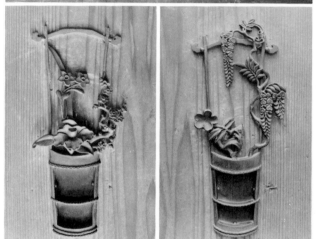

Fig. 18. Metal fixtures in New Palace, Katsura Detached Palace.

lend the building a sumptuous aspect (figs. 17, 18). Outside is a wide veranda, at the outer edge of which stand paper sliding screens. Just behind these runs a splendid handrail (pl. 10). But when these screens are opened, the view consists mostly of lawn, the pond visible only in the distance. The lawn was used for the game of *kemari*, a traditional and genteel form of kickball played by courtiers. But the lack of any garden view worthy of the name seems to have allowed the designer to concentrate his attention entirely on interior design. Then, for a place to view the garden, perhaps while sipping tea, the Shōkintei pavilion was built on a spot with a better view, and it was there that the designer focussed his efforts to establish harmony between interior and exterior space (pl. 12).

At the northeast of the shoin complex is the Palanquin Entry (Mikoshiyose). The design is stylized, however, with a post in the middle that made it impossible for the palanquin to be actually carried within the building itself as was the custom. The space is thought to have been named in keeping with earlier practice and was not meant to be used as such. The path of cut stone leading to it is famous (pl. 9; fig. 19). After passing under the Middle Gate, the path leads on a straight diagonal to the Palanquin Entry. To either side of the path, large and small stepping stones have been placed here and there. This mixture of rectilinearity and irregularity constitutes a kind of abstract art, and it is reiterated elsewhere in the villa. It represents a marriage of beauty and practicality. But rather than having been conceived as such from the first, this complex design seems to have been the result of various additions and changes over time.

The harmony of architecture and nature achieved at the Katsura Detached Palace is perhaps best expressed at the Shōkintei teahouse and surrounding garden. The pavilion is located on the east side of the central pond, directly across from the shoin complex. To the north is a small inlet with two islands, known as Ama no Hashidate, connected by a stone bridge. The main pond and the inlet were originally entirely separate. In later years the land between them was dug away and a large vermilion-lacquered bridge was added in its place, but this has since disappeared as well, save for minor vestiges. The inlet was personally designed by Toshitada, who gathered a variety of rocks for the purpose and devoted considerable care to their placement. The resulting design is quite different from that of the main pond. The Ama no Hashidate ("Bridge of Heaven") islands are meant to recall the famous scenic spot by the same name near the home of the mother of Toshitada, the second Hachijō prince, but that at Katsura is too stylized to reflect the appearance of its namesake (figs. 20, 21). The Ama no Hashidate motif was frequently used at the time, but Toshitada is said to have been motivated to use it more from a sense of filial piety toward his mother than anything else. The view of the Shōkintei from the far bank, across the tip of the Ama no Hashidate (pl. 13), and that from the Ama no Hashidate itself (pl. 12) are particularly beautiful.

The Shōkintei teahouse is built in a rustic style with a thatched roof. The main facade of the structure faces north, with the L-shaped Ichi no Ma as the main room and the Ni no Ma anteroom next to it at the east (fig. 23). The tearoom is appended to the rear. The Ichi no Ma was meant as a place for taking the customary meal after the tea ceremony, but it too has a hearth for making tea set into the floor matting in one corner. Shelves are hung above (fig. 22). Both hearth and shelves were added for the practical purpose of keeping prepared food warm, but their placement in the shadows around the corner from the decorative alcove shows artistic inspiration as well.

The eaves over the northern facade facing the pond have been elongated to cover the large outdoor hearth located di-

Fig. 20. Photograph of Ama no Hashidate in Miyazu, Kyoto Prefecture.
Fig. 21. Ama no Hashidate and Shōkintei teahouse, Katsura Detached Palace.

Fig. 19. Path leading to Palanquin Entry, Katsura Detached Palace.

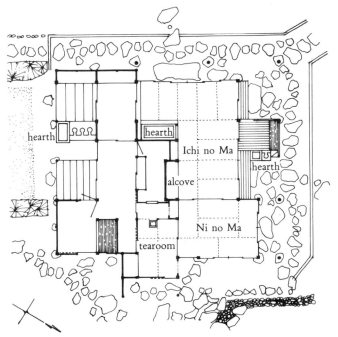

Fig. 22. Ichi no Ma of Shōkintei teahouse, Katsura Detached Palace.

rectly in front of the Ichi no Ma (pl. 14). Refreshments were prepared both here and at the other hearth to the rear of the Ichi no Ma. Despite the fact that food might normally be expected to be prepared out of sight in the rear of a building, several structures at Katsura Palace have hearths in front. This derives from the philosophy of tea. In the same way that tea is to be prepared directly in front of the participants during the ceremony, so is food to be prepared where all can observe the process. This is the highest courtesy the host can afford his guests. The use of this design in buildings at Katsura is thought to have been initiated by Toshitada himself. The overhanging eaves were probably built extra long so that the tea ceremony could be held even in inclement weather. Rain brings out the luster of each garden rock, further improving the beauty of the teahouse surroundings. Likewise, the various types of moss tend to fade after days in the sun, but recover their deep greens after a rainfall. Rainy days are actually the best times to view the garden, and the teahouse was designed accordingly.

PERFECTION IN A MOUNTAIN VILLA—THE SHUGAKUIN

The Shugakuin Detached Palace was built by the shogunate and presented to Retired Emperor Gomizunoo to allay his anger at Tokugawa interference in his affairs. Adroitly blended into the forest on the lower slope on Mount Hiei at the northeast of Kyoto, it presents a distinct contrast to Katsura Palace, which was constructed at about the same time in a completely man-made environment on damp lowlands by the Katsura River at the southeast.

The palace is composed of three separate complexes—the Upper, Middle, and Lower Villas—with the Upper Villa having the most majestic scenery, including a large pond made by building an embankment and damming a nearby stream (fig. 24). The island in the middle of the pond was the summit of a

Fig. 23. Plan of Shōkintei teahouse, Katsura Detached Palace.

Fig. 24. Yokuryūchi pond seen from Rin'untei pavilion, Shugakuin Detached Palace.

hill before the area was submerged. On a hillock above the pond sits the Rin'untei pavilion (pl. 15), from which point the entirety of the pond can be viewed against the peaks of Mount Atago in the background—another fine example of the "borrowed scenery" landscape technique. Though large in area, the pond itself is quite simple and pleasant. It has no rocks of eccentric shape that call attention to themselves. In the past, a small teahouse called the Shishisai used to stand on the opposite shore from the Rin'untei, and boats used to go between them, but nothing remains of it today save the marks of the foundation. Azaleas have been planted in profusion on the back slope of the pond's dam and pruned to the same height so as to completely obscure its actual function.

No other garden in Japan shows such effective exploitation of the natural features of the site or "borrows" the surrounding scenery on such a grand scale. In its perfect integration of architecture into multiple garden vistas, the Shugakuin is perhaps the best expression of the Japanese search for harmony between man and his natural environment.

AN EDO-PERIOD DAIMYO VILLA—THE RINSHUNKAKU

As the peace that marked the Edo period (1600–1867) progressed, more and more daimyos began building country retreats as places of relaxation. Much of this architecture was constructed in the rusticated and fanciful sukiya style. The genial atmosphere of these residences was well in keeping with the relative freedom from conflict the daimyos had come to enjoy. But the proprietors of these villas were nevertheless military men, and their residences consequently contrasted in some respects with structures like the Katsura and Shugakuin palaces, whose residents were royalty.

The Rinshunkaku, located within the Sankeien park in Yokohama, is the finest of the relatively few daimyo villas still remaining. The complex was originally built in what is now Wakayama Prefecture, and was moved to Yokohama after one intermediate relocation. Its builder was Tokugawa Yorinobu (1602–71), the second lord of Wakayama Castle and a member of the shogunal family. He chose as the site for his villa project a place called Iwade on the Ki River, twenty-five kilometers to the east of Wakayama City. As it required a full day simply to reach the villa, each visit represented a considerable time commitment. Yorinobu would also stop there on the regular trips to and from Edo that were required of all daimyos.

The Rinshunkaku is comprised of three buildings arranged in a stepped plan. The main structure, Building Two (Dainioku), now spans a pond (pl. 16), but was originally built out over the Ki River. Its position relative to Building Three (Daisan'oku; to the left in our illustration) used to be different as well, with the latter originally located behind the former. In front of both buildings, and visible from either, was a natural outcropping of rock that fulfilled the same function as hillocks built artificially in gardens to suggest mountains. Because of its distance from the city, then, the Rinshunkaku was able to incorporate natural elements such as the Ki River and rock groupings into its design instead of requiring artificial substitutes. And the villa originally used "borrowed scenery" as well, with a mountain of such majesty as to be called the "Mount Fuji of Ki Province" visible from the seat of honor, directly before the decorative alcove in the most important room in the complex, the Jōdan no Ma of Building Two.

It has been only a little over sixty years since the villa complex was moved to its present location. During the relocation process the pond was dug and Building Two was rebuilt over it, much as it had been over the Ki River. Building Three was repositioned to take advantage of the pond view, the focal center of the new configuration.

Fig. 25. Eastern facade of the Sumiya.

Fig. 26. Interior of the Sumiya.

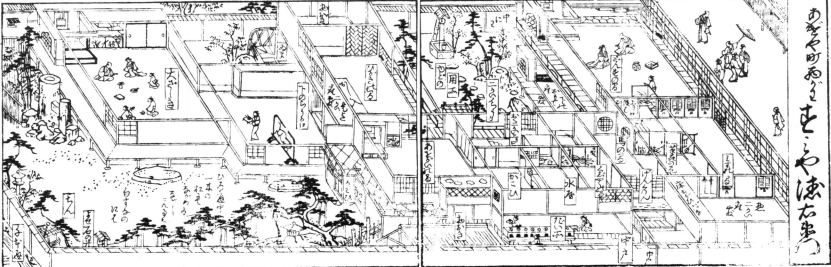

Fig. 27. Contemporary drawing of the Sumiya.

But the interior appearance of the buildings has not been altered. The Jōdan no Ma of Building Two (pl. 17) is composed in a manner typical of the shoin style, with a large decorative alcove and a subsidiary alcove side by side on the back wall. The entire space is raised one step to suggest its importance in the architectural hierarchy. But elements of the more fanciful sukiya style have been added as well—the room lacks the unbroken frieze rail that runs along the upper walls of orthodox shoin spaces, and the ceiling battens are fancifully arranged in perpendicular groupings rather than running the ceiling length in parallel.

Observed overall, the sukiya style of the Rinshunkaku shows stronger shoin influences than that of Katsura Palace, and this suggests a difference in the architectural philosophies of the military and the court. But in comparison to the rigid shoin style of the Ninomaru Palace of Nijō Castle, the Rinshunkaku has clearly moved much closer to the design ideals seen in the work of the princes Hachijō at Katsura.

ARCHITECTURE OF THE ENTERTAINMENT DISTRICT—THE SUMIYA

When the military regime of the Tokugawa was first established in the early seventeenth century, it severely curtailed trends toward luxury in the houses of the common people. As time went on, though, the military as a class found itself increasingly strapped financially, while members of the commoner stratum came into greater and greater wealth. Already by the end of the same century, the houses of some commoners had become quite opulent, shogunal sumptuary laws notwithstanding. Particularly in the "gay quarters," a place for not only prostitution but also social gatherings among the wealthy, popular architecture flourished and new and creative variations appeared constantly. By contrast, the reserved architecture of the warrior class began to show signs of artistic stagnation.

The difference between the architecture of the pleasure quarters and that of the military is clearly seen in the Sumiya in Kyoto's Shimabara entertainment district (figs. 25–27). The Sumiya is, in fact, the only surviving example of its type. In houses such as this, the class distinctions between warrior and commoner were ignored—the samurai was required to leave his sword on a rack outside before entering. Each residence had a spacious ōhiroma room as the center of its public activities. This would open onto a garden, that of each house showing off its own creative variations in landscaping technique. The ōhiroma of the Sumiya (pl. 18) was reconstructed after a destructive fire, but the restoration was made after the original conception.

Removing the sliding paper screens of the ōhiroma reveals a flat, gravel-covered garden with a hillock at the left supporting a rock grouping. Around the hillock an ancient pine known as the "Reclining Dragon" used to wreath its branches. Nothing but the trunk of the "Reclining Dragon" remains, but the original concept has been re-created with a number of small pines. The flat court can be likened to the surface of a lake, and the scene may in fact have been meant to re-create the famous Pine of Karasaki that snakes out over the shore of Lake Biwa to the east of Kyoto. The garden-ōhiroma complex at the Sumiya provided an ideal environment for opulent amusements, despite the building's exiguous urban site.

The aesthetics of the tea ceremony also exerted a powerful influence on the architecture of the pleasure quarters. At the Sumiya, for example, there is a tearoom on the second floor and a free-standing teahouse, of a later date, in the garden. The latter is approached via its own garden path (roji), along which guests walked to compose their minds prefatory to the tea ceremony proper.

There is also an enclosed garden court on the premises that

Fig. 28. Garden at Ryōanji seen from abbot's quarters.

shows the influence of tea taste in, for example, the use of a stone basin (*chōzubachi*) for washing the hands before drinking tea (pl. 19). Here again, the small garden court has been designed as a continuation of the interior space of the room from which it is viewed.

THE INFLUENCE OF MEDIEVAL ZEN TEMPLE ARCHITECTURE

We have seen that, through history, traditional Japanese residential architecture has been of two major types, the shinden style, which had its heyday in the eleventh century, and the shoin style, which reached maturity in the seventeenth. Each was accompanied by characteristic garden designs. The shoin style was further divided into the strictly orthodox style and its sukiya variation, the latter being strongly influenced by tea taste. And though elements of both shoin and the sukiya continue to be seen today, it is the sukiya style that has exerted the greatest influence on modern Japanese-style residential architecture.

The transition from the shinden to the shoin style by and large occurred in the medieval period, that is, the thirteenth through the sixteenth centuries. But despite these undercurrents of change, the medieval period was on the surface a dark age for Japanese residences. The reason for this was primarily economic. The court aristocracy, which had enjoyed preeminence in the Heian period, became progressively impoverished as their political prerogatives were arrogated by the rising military class, and much of their land—their primary source of

income—was usurped. But until peace was finally achieved in the seventeenth century, the warrior clans were too embroiled in wars with each other to build villas like those of the later daimyos of the Edo period.

During the medieval era, the burden of sustaining the nation's cultural activity was borne principally by Zen monks. One of their accomplishments was developing new styles of garden design, the most remarkable of which was the "dry landscape" (*karesansui*). These new gardens, which used fine gravel instead of water, would be constructed in front of the abbot's quarters (*hōjō*) and sometimes the monks' residence of a Zen temple. As these gardens were enclosed within earthen walls and were quite small in scale, trees were eschewed in favor of rocks, which were used expressively.

The most famous of these dry landscape gardens is at Ryōanji temple in Kyoto (fig. 28). There, the garden rectangle is composed simply of white gravel and a number of rocks. No greenery is used save for touches of moss at the bases of the rock groupings. This extremely spare composition prefigures modern abstract art. Some who have viewed it interpret the gravel as the sea and the rocks as islands within it. One of the most intriguing recent theories is that the rock placement represents the stars of the constellation Cassiopeia, as reflected in water. The rock arrangement does, in fact, bear an uncanny resemblance to a mirror image of that star group (fig. 29).

The Ryōanji garden is meant to be viewed from a fixed location—the middle of the south row of rooms in the abbot's

quarters. Seated there, one can fully appreciate the overall design conception (fig. 28). This method of garden viewing is vastly different from both that of the Heian period, when one might enjoy the landscape from a boat in the pond, and that of the Edo period, when it was the fashion to observe the garden scenery while strolling around the pond periphery. Some of these dry landscape gardens make use of large rocks said to resemble cranes or tortoises, both of which are associated in Japan with good fortune. Others use a tall and narrow rock to represent a waterfall and have other rocks on both sides to suggest a ravine. Here again, water is symbolized rather than actually used. This is very similar in concept to another of the major artistic contributions of Zen culture, ink painting, which uses nothing but the tones of the ink itself to create a statement that is sparse yet expressive.

The Zen rock garden exerted a powerful influence on the gardens of shoin-style architecture in and after the seventeenth century. The landscaping of Nijō Castle's Ninomaru Palace (pl. 8) and the rocks at the side of the pond beside Katsura's Shōkintei pavilion (pl. 12) are both cases in point. The Nijō garden shows further development, however, in that it can be viewed from any building in the structure, rather than from a single point as at Ryōanji. The garden path leading to the Shōkintei at Katsura remains more firmly linked to the earlier, Zen garden conception because it has large rocks set down at predetermined points where the viewer is meant to pause and appreciate the garden scenery.

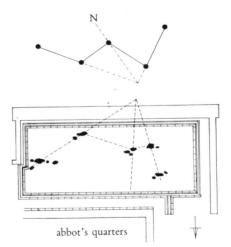

Fig. 29. Cassiopeia constellation compared with rock arrangement of garden at Ryōanji (from Nozaki Sōichi's *Kokoro no kiseki*).

So too is Zen influence found in the architecture and gardens of teahouses, which began to be frequently built in the sixteenth century. The teahouse is, of course, not a residence *per se*, but simply a building in which to perform the tea ceremony. As the tea ceremony itself was influenced by Zen beliefs, teahouses, like Zen gardens, have much in common with Zen ink paintings in their sparse simplicity (fig. 30). We have seen how the rough posts and farmhouse-style earthen walls of the teahouse were then taken into shoin structures to bring about the sukiya style.

It was thus the Zen institution that took the cultural initiative in the medieval period, when the court and military were sunk in a "dark age" of poverty and strife. And despite the abstruse philosophy underlying Zen, its teachings gradually came to exert a powerful influence on the contemporary ruling strata. Likewise the tea ceremony, molded by Zen concepts, made itself profoundly felt among the upper levels of society even though it had originated among the lower classes as an expression of opposition to the court and military aristocracy. Zen went on to become a driving force behind the military-centered culture that arose in the seventeenth century. Seen in this light, the influence and value of the medieval Zen institution was exceedingly great, a fact to which Japan's residences and gardens bear eloquent witness.

Fig. 30. Alcove in Myōkian teahouse, Kyoto.

Bibliography

Asano, Kiichi (photographs), and Takakura, Gisel (commentary). *Japanese Gardens Revisited*. Adapted by Frank Davies and Hirokuni Kobatake. Tokyo and Rutland, Vt.: Tuttle, 1973.

Blaser, Werner. *Japanese Temples and Tea Houses*. New York: Dodge, 1956.

Bring, Mitchell, and Wayembergh, Josse. *Japanese Gardens: Design and Meaning*. New York: McGraw-Hill, 1981.

Drexler, Arthur. *The Architecture of Japan*. New York: Museum of Modern Art, 1966.

Engle, Heinrich. *The Japanese House: A Tradition for Contemporary Architecture*. Tokyo and Rutland, Vt.: Tuttle, 1964.

Futagawa, Yukio (photographs), and Ito, Teiji (text). *The Roots of Japanese Architecture*. Translated by Paul Konya. New York: Harper and Row, 1963.

Hashimoto, Fumio. *Architecture in the Shoin Style: Japanese Feudal Residences*. Translated and adapted by H. Mack Horton. Japanese Arts Library, vol. 10. Tokyo and New York: Kodansha International and Shibundo, 1981.

Hayakawa, Masao. *The Garden Art of Japan*. Translated by Richard L. Gage. Heibonsha Survey of Japanese Art, vol. 28. New York and Tokyo: Weatherhill and Heibonsha, 1973.

Hayashiya, Tatsusaburo; Nakamura, Masa; and Hayashiya, Seizo. *Japanese Arts and the Tea Ceremony*. Translated and adapted by Joseph P. Macadam. Heibonsha Survey of Japanese Art, vol. 15. New York and Tokyo: Weatherhill and Heibonsha, 1974.

Hirai, Kiyoshi. *Feudal Architecture of Japan*. Translated and adapted by Hiroaki Sato and Jeannine Ciliotta. Heibonsha Survey of Japanese Art, vol. 13. New York and Tokyo: Weatherhill and Heibonsha, 1973.

Ishimoto, Yasuhiro. *Katsura: Tradition and Creation in Japanese Architecture*. Texts by Walter Gropius and Kenzo Tange. Translated by Charles Terry. New Haven: Yale University Press, 1960.

Ito, Teiji. *The Elegant Japanese House: Traditional Sukiya Architecture*. New York and Tokyo: Walker and Weatherhill, 1969.

———. *The Japanese Garden: An Approach to Nature*. Photographs by Takeji Iwamiya. Translated by Donald Richie. New Haven and London: Yale University Press, 1972.

———. *Space and Illusion in the Japanese Garden*. Photographs by Sosei Kuzunishi. Translated and adapted by Ralph Friedrich and Masajiro Shimamura. New York and Tokyo: Weatherhill and Tankosha, 1973.

———, with Paul Novograd. "The Development of Shoin-style Architecture." In *Japan in the Muromachi Age*, edited by John W. Hall and Takeshi Toyoda. Berkeley: University of California Press, 1977.

Iwao, Seiichi, ed. *Biographical Dictionary of Japanese History*. Translated by Burton Watson. Tokyo and New York: Kodansha International, 1978.

Kirby, John B. *From Castle to Teahouse: Japanese Architecture of the Momoyama Period*. Tokyo and Rutland, Vt.: Tuttle, 1962.

Kuck, Loraine. *The World of the Japanese Garden*. Photography by Takeji Iwamiya. New York and Tokyo: Walker and Weatherhill, 1968.

Morse, Edward. *Japanese Homes and Their Surroundings*. 1896. Reprint. Tokyo and Rutland, Vt.: Tuttle, 1972.

Naitō, Akira. *Katsura: A Princely Retreat*. Photography by Takeshi Nishikawa. Translated by Charles S. Terry. Tokyo and New York: Kodansha International, 1977.

Okawa, Naomi. *Edo Architecture: Katsura and Nikko*. Photography by Chuji Hirayama. Translated and adapted by Alan Woodhull and Akito Miyamoto. Heibonsha Survey of Japanese Art, vol. 20. New York and Tokyo: Weatherhill and Heibonsha, 1975.

Ota, Hirotaro, ed. *Traditional Japanese Architecture and Gardens*. Tokyo: Kokusai Bunka Shinkokai, 1966 (condensed ed., 1972).

Paine, Robert T., and Soper, Alexander C. *The Art and Architecture of Japan*. 3rd ed. New York: Penguin Books, 1981.

Sadler, A. L. *A Short History of Japanese Architecture*. 1941. Reprint. Tokyo and Rutland, Vt.: Tuttle, 1963.

Shigemori, Kanto. *Japanese Gardens: Islands of Serenity*. Tokyo: Japan Publications, 1971.

Tazawa, Yutaka, ed. *Biographical Dictionary of Japanese Art*. Tokyo and New York: Kodansha International, 1981.

定価3,800円
in Japan